BIOLOGY Field Notes

Be an OCTOPUS Expert

by
Noah Leatherland

Minneapolis, Minnesota

Credits
All images are courtesy of Shutterstock.com, unless otherwise specified. With thanks to Getty Images, Thinkstock Photo, and iStockphoto.

Recurring – Milano M, vectorplus, The_Pixel, yana shypova, Anna Frajtova. Doctor Character throughout – NotionPic. Cover – Anna Frajtova, Baksiabat, Andrea Izzotti, vectorplus, The_Pixel, Milano M. 4–5 – ennar0, Henner Damke. 6–7 – Aerial-motion, udomsook, Vladimir Turkenich. 8–9 – MattiaATH, Konstantin Novikov. 10–11 – K.Pock Pics, Shpatak, Yacob Hay Yacobi. 12–13 – George P Gross, Gennaro DiBs. 14–15 – MF Choi, Sean Lema, Sean Lema, RMMPPhotography, Menno Schaefer. 16–17 – Vittorio Bruno, Alexey Masliy. 18–19 – Gerald Robert Fischer, Amy Devine. 20–21 – Matt Wilson/Jay Clark, NOAA NMFS AFSC., Public domain, via Wikimedia Commons, Bass Supakit, scubadesign. 22–23 – Olga Visavi, ennar0.

Bearport Publishing Company Product Development Team
President: Jen Jenson; Director of Product Development: Spencer Brinker; Managing Editor: Allison Juda; Associate Editor: Naomi Reich; Associate Editor: Tiana Tran; Art Director: Colin O'Dea; Designer: Kim Jones; Designer: Kayla Eggert; Product Development Assistant: Owen Hamlin

Library of Congress Cataloging-in-Publication Data is available at www.loc.gov or upon request from the publisher.

ISBN: 979-8-88916-965-9 (hardcover)
ISBN: 979-8-89232-484-7 (paperback)
ISBN: 979-8-89232-120-4 (ebook)

© 2025 BookLife Publishing
This edition is published by arrangement with BookLife Publishing.

North American adaptations © 2025 Bearport Publishing Company. All rights reserved. No part of this publication may be reproduced in whole or in part, stored in any retrieval system, or transmitted in any form or by any means, electronic, mechanical, photocopying, recording, or otherwise, without written permission from the publisher. Bearport Publishing is a division of Chrysalis Education Group.

For more information, write to Bearport Publishing, 5357 Penn Avenue South, Minneapolis, MN 55419.

CONTENTS

Meet the Biologist............4
An Octopus's Body............6
Squeeze and Swim............8
Under the Sea...............10
Rocky Homes.................12
Dinnertime..................14
Tricky Ink..................16
Blending In.................18
Life Cycle..................20
Outstanding Octopuses.......22
Glossary....................24
Index.......................24

Being an octopus **expert** is a lot of work. I filled this notebook with everything I know about octopuses. Will you read it? Together, we can find out even more!

AN OCTOPUS'S BODY

Octopuses are known for their eight long arms. These arms help octopuses crawl along rocks and sand. Each arm has two rows of suckers. The suckers help octopuses stick to things and grab objects.

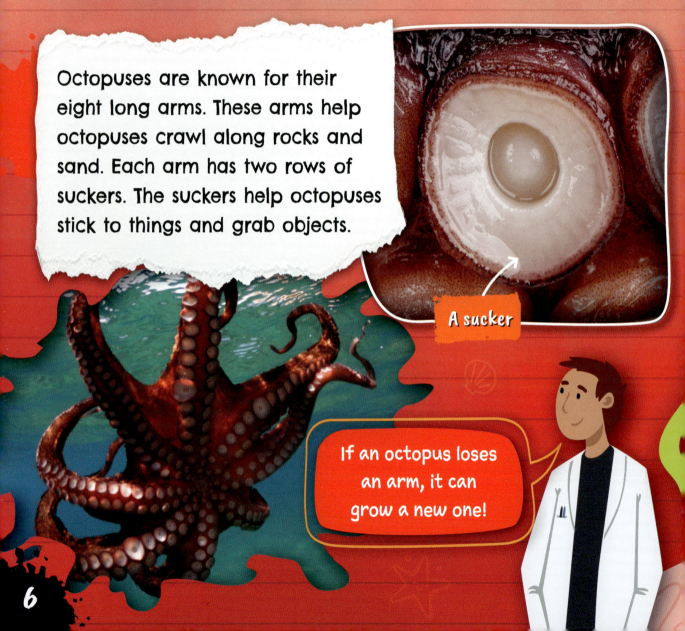

A sucker

If an octopus loses an arm, it can grow a new one!

Each octopus arm has a group of **nerves** that acts as a small brain. These nerves help the arms move on their own. Including the main brain in an octopus's head, that makes nine octopus brains total!

An octopus's main brain is shaped like a doughnut.

SQUEEZE AND SWIM

The central body of an octopus is called the mantle. Octopuses have no bones. This lets them squeeze into small spaces and through tight gaps.

Mantle

Octopuses have blue blood and three hearts.

An octopus's mantle has two holes. One sucks water in, and the other shoots the water out. This pushes the octopus through the water as it swims.

Octopuses can swim up to 25 miles per hour (40 kph).

UNDER THE SEA

There are around 300 kinds of octopuses. They are found in waters all over the world. Many octopuses live at the very bottom of the sea. Some live in **shallow** waters near the beach.

Most octopuses live in warm waters.

Octopuses live in homes called dens for a couple of weeks at a time. These homes are usually found near **coral reefs**. Most octopuses live alone. They are very protective of their dens.

ROCKY HOMES

Octopuses make their own dens. First, an octopus finds a small hole. Then, it uses its long, strong arms to stack rocks and other hard objects around the space.

Octopuses close their dens by blocking any openings with rocks.

Octopuses spend most of their time in their dens. They may come out at night to hunt for food. Sometimes, octopuses leave their dens to build new ones.

DINNERTIME

What do octopuses eat? These eight-armed animals feed on other sea creatures, such as sea snails, crabs, shrimp, and even other octopuses. They use their long arms to catch their **prey**. Then, they bring the meal to their beak, which they use to take a **venomous** bite.

A shrimp

A sea snail

A crab

Octopus beaks also help them crunch through animals with hard shells.

Octopuses have many **predators**. In the deep ocean, they have to look out for sharks, whales, and dolphins. Birds and sea otters hunt octopuses that live in shallow water.

A dolphin

A sea otter

TRICKY INK

Some octopuses make a dark liquid called ink. They can squirt this ink into the water, creating a thick, black cloud.

Ink

Ink makes it hard for other animals to see. Octopuses use their ink to confuse predators and give themselves time to escape. While hunting, some octopuses use their ink to stop their prey from seeing them coming.

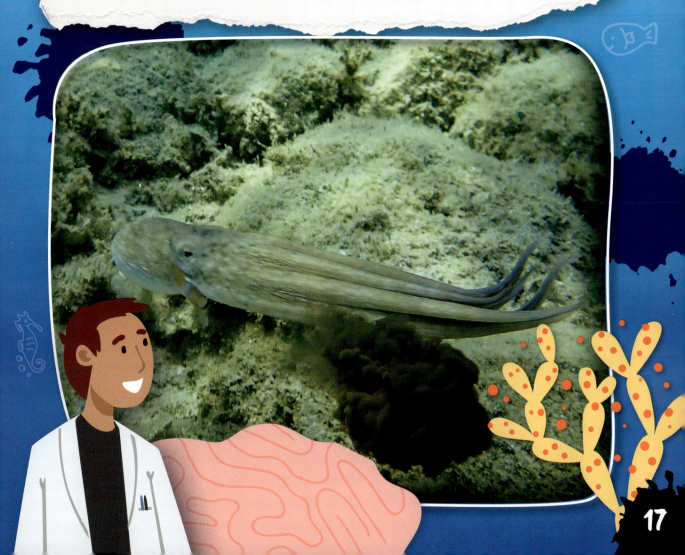

BLENDING IN

Ink isn't the only thing octopuses use to hide and hunt. They can also **camouflage** themselves. They blend in with the things around them, such as rocks and sand.

Can you spot the octopus?

Even more surprising, octopuses can change the color and feel of their skin. They do this to match their surroundings. These tricky animals can look like rocks and feel like lumps of coral.

How about now?

LIFE CYCLE

Octopuses start their life cycles as eggs. They hatch as little **larvae** (LAHR-vee). These babies grow and are on their way to becoming juveniles. When they are about one or two years old, juvenile octopuses turn into adults.

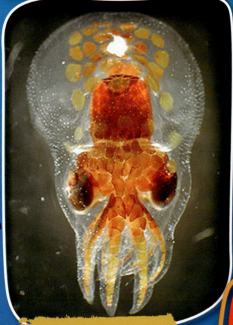

An octopus larva

A juvenile

A life cycle includes the different stages of an animal's life.

Eggs

Some octopuses can live for up to five years.

When they get old, mother octopuses lay eggs. Sometimes, they have thousands at a time. A mother keeps her eggs safe for four to eight weeks. Once her babies have hatched safely, the mother octopus dies.

OUTSTANDING OCTOPUSES

There are so many outstanding things about octopuses! I hope you've enjoyed learning about these eight-armed creatures.

GLOSSARY

biologist a person who studies and knows a lot about living things

camouflage a covering or coloring that makes animals blend into their surroundings

coral reefs groups of rocklike structures formed from the skeletons of sea animals

expert someone who knows a lot about a subject

larvae baby octopuses that have just hatched from eggs

nerves parts of the body that send messages from the brain to other parts of the body

predators animals that hunt other animals for food

prey animals that are hunted and eaten by other animals

shallow not very deep

venomous able to attack with a poisonous bite

INDEX

arms 6–7, 12, 14, 22
brains 7
dens 11–13
eggs 20–21
ink 16–18
larvae 20
ocean 15
predators 15–17
prey 10, 14–15
sea 10, 14–15
skin 19
suckers 6